Table of Contents

Access all available resources

Resume and social profiles

Treat it like a project

Introduction

If today is the day you find yourself in a conversation at work that starts with;

"Sorry (insert your name). Your job no longer exists", then this book is for you.

If today is the day you are thinking that this might happen to you, then this book is for you too.

This book has been written by someone (me) who knows what it feels like to being told that my job no longer exists (twice!) and survived, but stumbled and fumbled her way through.

It doesn't matter what our respective work or industries call it – being told our jobs no longer exists can come in many forms and under the guise of many different terms. Some people call it being laid off, made redundant, being retrenched and made unemployed. I prefer the term becoming 'underemployed'.

Ultimately it all means the same thing.

What we were doing for a job when we woke up this morning is no longer available to us – well certainly not in the exact same circumstances that we were used to.

And it can happen for many reasons – company restructures, jobs being outsourced, companies in liquidation, future automation of tasks, business maturity cycles where new skill sets are required resulting in the company / organisation no longer needing what you have to offer.

Ouch!

<u>Change is here</u>

Being told that your job no longer exists means change is here.

Life as it you knew it has changed.

Where you go to work, what you earn (at least temporarily), where you find your challenge, your purpose, your identity, what your daily routine is, your circle of friends and colleagues – all can get thrown up in the air and land back down in a muddy puddle of confusion and uncertainty.

And the change doesn't just affect one area of your life, it may impact other areas – your health, your self esteem, your identity, your finances, your relationships, your support circle etc. Some of these positively and some negatively.

It's wishful to think it is simply about 'dusting ourselves off and starting again', although that is what ultimately we need to do. To make sure the change works and is a positive experience, we must become the master of change for our own lives.

We need to make this change work and work in our favour, no matter how hard or unwelcome it may be.

I believe there are three stages of change we go through when we lose access to the job we had;

1. We must fully understand the change and recognize that it is happening right now **(Adapt)**
2. We must say goodbye to the old and unplug from the current workplace**(Part)**
3. We must get ready and make room for the new**(Restart)**

How well we **Adapt. Part. Restart** will define our success and how quickly we can move on.

How do I know this? Because I have been on both sides of the fence on this issue – I have been told my job no longer exists twice in my 20+ career and I have had to tell others, their jobs no longer exist, so I get it!

But in the moment it happens, even if you did see it coming, there are things you can do that will help your mindset, attitude, energy and perspective to turn it into a positive experience rather than make a frantic run towards a cliff.

In that split second you get the news, however it is delivered to you, your JOB has changed. Whatever it was, it is no longer. The decision has been made. That's the cold hard fact.

It's done.

So being able to **Adapt** to that news is your first challenge. We must fully understand the change and recognize that it is happening right now. It's happening to you.

The second challenge is to undertake the series of logistical steps to 'unplug' or **Part** from your ex or the the company/organisation in a way that is empowering for you. This can be emotionally tough to do.

And thirdly, the final challenge is to be able to be in the right head and heart space to hit the **Restart** button and start focussing forward on what's next for you and taking the necessary actions.

In this moment, know that you do have a JOB. The JOB is you. Looking after you, your best interests, your dreams, your plans, your wants and your immediate and future needs.

In this moment, you become your own boss again. Your role is to be looking out for you and what you need, what you need to do next and how you can turn this unexpected news into something that propels your forward, not backwards.

Consider yourself 'self employed'. Employed by you.

You are employing yourself to find and make your way through this change and into the next opportunity for your life and your career. You are now in charge of managing this change and it may well become one of those defining moments in your life.

So just for one moment, let's imagine that we are seeing the loss of our job as a coin toss:

Heads it is **devastating**

Tails it is **liberating**

Which side of the coin is it or will it be for you? There's power in what you call it and I regard this as one of the key power moves you can make.

This book will provide you with some rock steady steps you can take as well as some proven 'power moves' you can do that will help you in different ways to move forward and handle the situation and the environment you now find yourself in.

This book is not written by human resource professionals or psychologists with PhDs in human behaviour or even career specialists. It is written from the wisdom and experience of people who have been there and been through it personally.

It is the culmination of wisdom from lessons learned and the 'lessons not learned' in the trial and error process in order to save your time and heartbreak.

I want to acknowledge here the courage and generosity of all those who have shared their stories with me on what they did, what they didn't do, what worked and where they stumbled and ultimately created their own breakthroughs that made it all possible to hit **Restart** and create a new future for themselves.

In this book, we boldly tell the truth and you may not agree with everything that is said and that's OK. My purpose in presenting this information is to be as truthful and transparent about what often happens in these situations to give you a chance to be as prepared as you can be.

Is every job loss situation different? **Probably.**

Are there some common themes happening? **Absolutely**.

"Absorb what is useful, discard what is useless and add what is specifically your own"

– Bruce Lee, Wisdom for The Way

And here's one truth to give you an idea if this book is right for you;

Being told your job no longer exists is personal – of course it is. The company is saying they no longer need you. To know this and accept this, but not dwell on this, will fast track your 'recovery'. Some people will say it's not personal and that is quite unhelpful. It actually helps to acknowledge that it is personal. It's personal because it is about and for you – it's all about you.

Another truth that I reveal in this book and it was one that caught me by surprise is the surprisingly and unexpected consequences of losing your job is being prepared to handle the reaction of others, at a time that you are probably just trying to work out how to handle it yourself!

All of sudden, it can feel less about you and more about other people.

The reaction of others, took me by surprise and I found myself spending an extraordinary amount of time, making others feel comfortable with what's going on. For the most part, the people around me were caring about me and trying to be supportive, but what became crystal clear to me is that 'me losing my job', made other people very uncomfortable – they didn't know what to say, they started to worry it would happen to them, some people even became a little judgemental and applying blame for what happened as their own coping mechanism – they were trying to make sense of it themselves.

So there is a ripple effect of this change and it can impact many people.

My Coin Toss On a Job Loss

My job loss experience is a story of two sides of the same coin.

Heads it was devastating (the first time)

Tails it was liberating (the second time)

The first time I was told my job no longer existed was devastating and it knocked the wind out of my sails. I let myself take a big 'self esteem' hit and I limped back into hiding feeling humiliated and ashamed. It was my dream job; I had been head hunted for it. I was loving it and I was just getting started, I had an amazing team, delivering amazing results and then the company decided to move the operation headquarters overseas and my local role (and some of the roles on my team) were no longer required. We were told one day in the boardroom, all of us together by an extremely nervous manager who had been given the job to deliver the message. I remember him distinctly gulping back at a bottle of water as he delivered the news. It was probably really hard for him looking back, but its one of those things that in the moment, I wasn't really listening to him. It was like the room had gone completely silent and all I could hear and see was him starting to talk and then reaching for his water bottle and the sound of the water gulping down this throat.

No judgment here on him. He was just doing his job, but it is funny what you remember about the moment it happens. It stays with you. :)

Ouch!

It hurt. It didn't seem logical. I wanted to argue. And it wasn't done very well. I was angry but most of all, I felt disappointed at having let my team down. As their leader, my role was to look after them and ensure their safety and well being and now I couldn't prevent the fact that some of them had just lost their jobs. And it was all my fault – at least that is what I thought at the time. This was the first unhelpful lie I told myself.

What could I have done that would have avoided this situation? Was there anything I could have done? How did I get it so wrong?

All the time I just assumed it was my fault. I wasn't thinking that this was a logical decision for the business to relocate overseas and that it was just strategy. That maybe that was all it was. I made it a disaster in my head and worse still in my heart. It wounded me to be the point where I never wanted to lead a team again. I was not good enough. I couldn't protect them.

The perspective I had was that it was all my fault. And that perspective made it very hard to move on and so it took me awhile to find my feet again. I took some time off, did some contracting to keep myself busy and occupied, before starting on a new career step doing much the same work, but in a different industry and enjoying some considerable success.

To this day, I remain good friends with my team members who lost their jobs that same day – it's kind of a bond we have – once you go through something like this, you have a connection on a different level. I am pleased to say that over the next few years, we all moved on to establish ourselves again and have been very successful. It comes up in conversation ever now and again, so we remember it, but it doesn't have any charge to it.

So did I see it coming. **No.**

Did I handle it well? **Not really**.

Did I understand what to do and how to get myself out of it. **Nope**.

Did I make it something it really wasn't? **Yes**

Did I make it harder for myself than it needed to be? **Absolutely**!

Then a funny thing happened. I started to run into other people who had been told their jobs no longer existed and I started to realise that we are not taught or educated how to handle this event. And it seemed to be much more common than we might think.

I have friends who have been made redundant three or four times in their career and they just accept it and are of course, disappointed when it happens again, but they get it now and recover quickly and move on. And I have other friends and colleagues who will never experience this event.

It is just so.

In writing this book, I tried to find out the statistics of the number of people who are laid off, retrenched, made redundant and it was difficult to obtain due to the complex nature of the reasons why companies let people go and remove jobs.

So my quantitative evidence for this book is purely experiential and gained from my interviews, but I know for sure, that if you are going through this experience, you are not alone. #Yana.

Now the second time it happened to me was in completely different circumstances.

I was in a senior management role with a multi-billion-dollar company and whilst the job and the company were sought after and well respected, I was desperately unhappy.

I was not feeling fulfilled and the challenge in the job had left me and as a result, my performance started to suffer. I never had a poor performance review ever and in fact, every year I would be given bonuses for my work and gradually promoted to heading up a department. This was a great accomplishment and I was very proud that I had done this, but it wasn't really me. It's hard to stay engaged with something if you are not connected with it. I liked the people I worked with and the company culture was one of the more empowering examples going around. But it just wasn't it for me. My problem was that I didn't listen to the whispers.

The whispers that the company was giving me about whether I really wanted to be there, the whispers in my own head that was saying leave and go do what you really want to do, the whispers in my soul that said you are enough just the way you are, you don't need more training or more experiences and that the world needs to see and hear your gifts – stop playing in this field and go explore and share with the world who you are and bring value to others.

So when you know that you have stayed too long in a job, it means that fear is driving you. My fears were loud and clear to me – what would I do if I left the company, how could I support myself, what job could I get. At the start of every week, I would rally myself and think this is the week I would be able to turn things around and find the new funk in my job that made me enjoy it more. It wasn't so much the job, the people or the company that was the issue. It was me, being too scared to act on what my heart was already saying.

And this is what I was telling myself every day

"This is good, but this isn't it. And this isn't you!"

About two years earlier I had started to embrace a mindfulness and daily meditation practice to help me centre and reduce the stress I was feeling from being somewhere that I knew I no longer belonged and didn't really want to be, but was too scared to move. I was fortunate to study and attend some Advanced courses with the amazing Dr Joe Dispenza in the US and Mexico, after my friend Julie bought us both tickets to one of his workshops in Melbourne and I found what I was looking for. I dived deep into learning how our minds work and how we can train our brains to create our compelling futures and the power of intention. It would be an understatement to say this had an impact on me and the way I started to think about my life changed. I started to meditate about what my life calling was, what I was here to do on the planet and what I wanted to have in my life. I started to change. And I started to move even further away from being in love with my job, but still couldn't find the courage to leave.

I had created in my meditation practice a way for me to let my mind be clear and get beyond my ego and allow myself to tap into what I knew was a higher source for me. In other words, I was getting the 'downloads' that I had a bigger game to play in this lifetime. It wasn't like it was all being laid out in front of me(which was a source of frustration got to be honest!), it was more of a sense or knowing that there was a different picture or intention than what I had created so far in my life for me.

Coming back from an Advanced course in Cancun with Dr Joe, for the next six months I would meditate most if not every day and focus on getting out of my own way. From a meditation point of view, it really meant I had to leave my body, my identity, who I was, what my job was and return back to a space of complete 'nothingness' or if you like a void. Some people refer to this as the present moment. By spending time in the present moment, I no longer was my past or my future. I was just now. Therefore, I was anything and everything. I was no longer defining myself based I what I had achieved in my career nor my perceived failing which is what I was experiencing and being reminded of everyday I went to work. I was just being present. This might sound a little 'woo woo' and I didn't always understand it, I just knew I felt so much better when I did this practice and that every time I tried to stay in the present and not in my uncertain future, I gained even more insight into what I should do.

At work I was fortunate to be part of an amazing leadership training conducted by the Authentic Leadership Institute by a guy called Nick Craig. It was during this course that we were all challenged to define our authentic leadership purpose. It was a tough exercise and I know many people found it challenging, but there were also a lot of breakthrough moments for people as they became very very clear on what their purpose was. My authentic leadership purpose I discovered from the work we did was to 'inspire the solutions and then get out of the way'.

This is what I felt I was doing in my current role, but I knew I wanted to do this on a bigger scale, play a bigger game if you like.

On December 1, 2014 I was at home and I realised I was done. I was done thinking and trying to work it all out. I realised I was trying to make it all perfect, before I would make the jump. I wanted to have everything lined up, my safety net in place and then I would make the big move and leave my job. But it hadn't happened. There was no net, no next job to go to, no overflowing bank account to fund my dreams – I hadn't been able to create anything. Well that's how it felt to me.

I needed to support my 'jump'.

Sitting on the lounge room floor I started to cry because I didn't know what else to do. Was all this meditation and mindfulness just a load of 'woo woo' after all? How come I could not make myself happy in the great job I had or manifest the next option for me? After all I was doing the work!

As the hot tears flowed, the room seemed to get really quiet. I am sure I could just about hear my own heartbeat. And then I had a profound realisation;

"Whilst I was waiting for all the things I wanted in my life to show up, the truth was the universe was waiting for me to show up and be open to receive everything I was asking for"

As Dr Joe Dispenza says, you have to get up like its already happened.

Now this may be in 'woo woo' land for some of you, but bear with me.

And if you can relate to what I am saying about my own experience, you will know that in these moments, there is always one more step you can take, just when you think you have done everything you need to, there's always another step, another action to take. And I realised that I needed to take the step and resign.

So on December 1, 2014, I was going to jump after all – without a safety net. Gee – it kind of felt good.

So I wrote out my resignation letter and took it in with me the next day to work, I was not feeling the 'high' of last night's revelation and actually felt sick to my stomach all day. Was I really going to do this? Am I crazy? My boss had previously scheduled a 4pm appointment for us on that day, so that's when I was going to tell her.

And you'll never guess what happened next. My boss came into my office and she sat down and before I could get a chance to hand in my resignation letter, she told me that I no longer had a job. This was pretty unusual as this company very rarely makes people redundant, so it was not commonplace.

It was obvious that she wasn't comfortable about having to tell me that my role no longer was required. I saw that in her eyes and heard it in her voice. As I heard her tell me, again that thing happened where it seems like the world stops and I thought I could hear my own heartbeat.

In that split second, it was like the cloud around me lifted. I smiled and told her it was all OK. I told her I agreed with the decision! And I was happy. Thank you.

That's right. I agreed. Why? The universe had been conspiring for me, reacting to my desire to do something new and it just manifested a way for me to do it and my safety net just appeared.

#boom!

That day, I was given a good payout that became the funding for my dream. I couldn't have designed it in any better way.

It was the right thing for me and the right thing for the business. Happy days all round.

I will never forget that moment in my lounge room when I had the realisation that I needed to take the jump without the safety net (inspire the solution) and jump (get out of my own way). It has been imprinted on me as one of the greatest lessons of my life and validation that what I was experiencing in my daily mindfulness practice had just materialised in front of me. I know it was because I took that final step of the night before by writing out my resignation letter and 'jumping' without the safety net.

Given I was so happy and my boss and the business was happy and in alignment, I said I wasn't going to hang around, that I was going to leave straightaway and organise a good time to come back and say goodbye to my team. So 15 minutes later, I collected my personal things from my office and left. In the ensuing days, I did get a chance to connect with my team and say goodbye and thank those people I wanted to express my thanks too and my new journey began on December 2, 2014.

And again, from that moment, I have attracted to me lots of people who have been through the same experience of being told their jobs no longer existed, albeit each and every one of us in different circumstances. I've been curious to say the least, to find out what they did to make it through and I can now share the lessons we all learnt with you here in this book.

I know that whilst our circumstances may differ, the lessons are the same.

Being told your job no longer exists is disruptive for sure, but it may well become a defining moment that you will never forget and set you on your true path.

The Moment It Happens

So if you have been told your job no longer exists, you'll remember that moment forever. And if it hasn't happened to you yet, but you are reading this because you think it might happen to you, then this book will help you get prepared for it.

If you are prepared, it will be a bit easier.

The conversation might go something like this;

- "(insert your name), we are making some changes, a restructure and your role unfortunately will no longer exist, we are really sorry……" and then their voices trail off and you are not really hearing anything that they say after that – at least for a split second.

The world goes quiet – you can hear your heartbeat!

Your head goes fuzzy – all its saying is 'what the **** do I do now?' What does this mean?

Or maybe it happened a bit like this;

- Today you turned up to work just like any other day and got called into a room with your boss and someone from HR and there was no eye contact when you arrived and you knew that something was about to happen and it was probably not going to be good.

Or

- Your company starts announcing the need to downsize due to downturn in economic viability, and they are particularly vague on details – you start to feel nervous.

Or

- There's an announcement (or even just a rumour) made at work, that redundancies are going to be offered, and you start to think whether you will be one of those people offered a redundancy and whether it's the right thing for you. Who else is going to take one?

Or

- You turn up to work and the sign says, business has closed and there's a phone number to call – this is definitely not good.

<u>Does it make a difference as to how your job was lost?</u>

Not really. The outcome is the same. That's the truth.

For some it is highly significant and a profound personal challenge to regain sure footing and move forward. For others, its little more than an inconvenience. And for others, it is a 'gift in disguise' and a chance of new beginnings.

In this book I am excluding any reference to losing your job through misconduct or poor performance. That's not what this book is about.

So my wish is that I can give you a heads up on what you may go through and by having some knowledge up front that it will help you to navigate your way back into a winning and confident position.

So let's outline what actually happens.

There are three key stages – Adapt. Part. Restart and I will explain what happens through each stage.

Along the way, there are some key tactics or I prefer to call them 'power moves' that you can make that will make it easier for you to move forward.

A word of caution: If this event has happened or is about to happen, you will be inundated with a lot of new information to process and manage. I recommend you get a notebook or create a file on your computer or use Notes on your phone to capture all this information and keep it all in the one spot. There are also some blank pages at the back of this book for your note taking as well. No excuses!

What to Do When You Are Told Your Job No Longer Exists

1. ADAPT

We must fully understand the change and recognize that it is happening right now

Awareness

Decision

Ask

Payout/package

Timing

2. PART

We must say goodbye to the old and unplug from the current workplace

Pause and get some perspective

Approach

Reaction (yours and others)

Take care of your needs

3. RESTART

We must get ready and make room for the new

Renew your focus

Explore all options

Seek more information

Take stock financially

Access all available resources

Resume and social profiles

Treat it like a project

Stage 1 - ADAPT

We must fully understand the change and recognize that it is happening right now

ADAPT stands for:

Awareness

Decision

Ask

Payout/package

Timing

Awareness

Know what it being said to you

It's important, that you become very aware of what's being said to you in the moment that your boss or someone else is giving you this message.

Stop and really listen. Take a few deep breaths so you are as present as you can be. Try to focus just on the now. Try not to get ahead of yourself and start the 'worry' process about your future and what you have to do next.

Too often we can hear the first few words someone is saying and we think we get the gist of what's about to be said and then we start to tune out and let our minds wander to where we think they are going with the conversation, rather than actually where they are going.

This is a time for listening to understand. Listening for clarity.

Have a pen and paper handy. Write down what they are saying – even if its jotting down some key words as you hear them. This will be important in the next few steps.

Try not to react at this point – hear them out.

Try not to get emotional, as this will make it even harder for you to stay aware of your surroundings and what is being said to you at this very time. I know this is hard too.

The most important thing to become aware of is that 'it just happened'. You have just been told your job no longer exists. It's happened. That's the key point to recognise and acknowledge and its not the time to do anything else, but let that sink in.

You certainly don't have to like it and be all 'Pollyanna' about it. In fact, it will probably bring up a sense of disbelief that it is happening now and that it is happening to you and you may be thinking already – why you? But rest assured, it has just happened and you need to become very aware of the situation you now find yourself in and start to prepare to react effectively.

At this time, you need to be fully AWARE, you don't need to fully ACCEPT it at this point. That will come a bit later on…

Decision

Hear the details of what is being said to you

A decision has been made about you and your future with your workplace. Know that. The decision has been made.

The decision you are hearing about right now has probably been through a review and series of discussions/meetings with your boss or HR personnel, so its highly likely the person who is informing you has known for a period of time, whether that is for 24 hours, 3 days, 3 weeks or 3 months or more, they will have known its coming and have prepared their approach to tell you.

You however, have not had that luxury of being prepared and it will probably come as a complete shock.

Now, not all of us are great at reacting in the moment. Some people are comfortable and react in alignment with who they are. And others, will react badly and not necessarily as their best selves. That's understandable – you have not had a chance to be prepared in most cases, so its OK, be yourself but know that the decision has been made.

What exactly is the decision? What are the details? Listen carefully. Write them down.

Ask

Now its your turn, take a breath and seek clarity by asking questions.

Ask for a pen and paper if you don't already have one. Jot down any questions you may have. Take your time.

If in the moment you are lost in what was or is being said, asked them to go back to the start or repeat it back so you can hear it again. Do not assume you heard it all correctly.

This is about checking for understanding. It is likely that your mind may have been sent off track after you heard that you no longer have a job and have missed some of the details, so it is really important (and vital) that you ask questions and get clarity.

You might have been given some papers outlining the details and told that all the information you need is contained in there for you to take away and read later. Whilst this is helpful, it can be a tactic to get this awkward conversation over with (for both parties) and to take some of the heat out of it. But don't let this sway you – if you have questions, you can ask them there and then.

Note: The answers you receive may not be satisfactory to you or even make any sense and you may feel slightly sceptic or at least unnerved, perhaps mistrusting even at this time, that's OK. But its no time to get into an argument. You do have a right to know why the decision was made and why you have been affected, but note that you may not be satisfied with the explanation you receive.

Example questions to ask at this time, could be;

Why was this decision made exactly?

Why was I chosen / Why me?

Do I have other options within the company?

Is this immediate? When do I have to leave?

<u>Stay calm</u>

It may not feel like it, but you are in fact the one that has some control right now and this is why. Organisations will have made this call long before you are hearing about it and the person charged with delivering the message, will likely be either under instruction for the conversation to go well or at least be delivered without drama and incidence.

We hope their intentions are fair and just, but we can't necessarily bank on that. By this I mean, they will prefer that it is done in a calm and professional manner and not be uncomfortable for them, knowing that it will be uncomfortable for you.

So they will want you to remain calm (for their sake, not necessarily yours, although this will help you down the track). So any reasonable HR person or boss will care about you and how this news will affect you, and will respect your right to ask questions and take a moment, rather than rush you out of the room with a piece of paper and a 'thank you for your contribution to our company' and a 'you will be missed'.

So take some control of the conversation and ask for any clarification you need.

Remember at this point you may feel a range of emotions – upset, scared, angry that is all natural and understandable, but try to contain these for now.

Package or payout

Am I being financially compensated for this decision?

In the heat of this moment, there will be quite a few thoughts rolling around in your head and it is highly likely and understandable that one of the most critical will be, what will be the financial impact to my life of this decision.

- Am I going to get paid out? If so, how much will that be? How long will that last?
- If so, how much will that be? How am I going to pay the bills without a job?
- I have bills to pay due tomorrow!
- My partner is out of work. This is going to be put a lot of pressure on my family.

The fair work laws and legislation differ significantly across countries, industries, government and private businesses and as such are not a topic for inclusion in this book. I strongly recommend you seek advice from your relevant department, association or union to know your rights (prior to this event occurring).

However, it is common for employees to receive some type of payout or package from their employer if their job has been terminated through no fault of the employee. The terms and conditions of this payout/package may include, but not limited to, the following:

- Lump sum payment based on years of service
- Discretionary payment
- Holiday leave entitlements
- Payout details from any employment related bonuses such as shares, car lease
- Reconciliation of superannuation
- Taxation calculations on any lump sum

What tends to happen in the moment, is that these figures may be explained to you verbally and go in one ear and out the other. If you don't receive it in writing, you should ask for a copy so that you can take it away with you and read it and absorb it and also then provide to your own financial advisor to check for accuracy and compliance with all the relevant regulations.

For most people, the loss of a job has the potential to significantly disrupt their financial positions, even if only for a short time and sometimes longer, so it is important to get this as clear so you can make effective and sound decisions in the coming days and weeks.

It is also possible, that the payout figure you receive, may well be the largest amount of money you have received in your lifetime in one lump sum and it needs to be managed with care. Your task is to make sure you have the information that the company/organisation is telling you in writing and take it away with you.

<u>Negotiate (where you can)</u>

A note about negotiation here. The company/organisation wants this conversation to go well and all parties find a mutually agreeable solution and move on. The benefits of being prepared for this conversation by knowing your rights beforehand, can help to put you in a sound position to negotiate your payout or conditions at this time.

I highly recommend this as a strategy if you are feeling confident and well informed about what grounds you may have to negotiate on – this is a power moment and it can work for you in your favour.

You should consider things such as:

- Provision of outplacement services at no cost to you, if not already provided
- Retainment of any entitlements such as shares, car leases
- Retainment of company provided materials – laptops, phones etc.
- Termination date, whether to stay or go and what's the timing
- Options for alternate jobs within the company, even at a lower salary level, if necessary

Timing

Do I stay or go? When do I have to leave?

Remember, this decision about your future has already been decided, so has the timing of your departure. However, this is also something that is often negotiable, refer previous point.

It will depend on your company/organisation.

They could be asking you to leave straight away i.e. that day.

They could ask you stay for a standard four weeks to give you some breathing space to start your job seeking and to do a handover to someone in their organisation – this is fairly common.

They could ask you to stay on for 3 or 6 months to finish a particular project or help with a transition to a new structure for example

Or they could offer you the choice – whatever works for you.

So do you stay or go? Hang around or take the package and run!

Again, this is a good choice to consider in advance if perhaps you thought this might happen to you.

For me, when it happened, I had no interest in hanging around. I left with grace and did not feel the need to stay. I left that day and caught up with my team and the people important to me in the ensuing days, outside of the work office and this was perfect for me. But everyone is different.

You might feel more comfortable, accepting a four week or longer notice and staying in your role whilst you take the necessary steps to start looking into what you might do next. This gives you a chance to say goodbye to people in your organisation and wrap things up in the way you want to do things. It can also be fairly tough to handle as people may feel uncomfortable around you and not know how to approach you, knowing that you have just been told you no longer have a job and may be upset about it. But if you have a good support network in your workplace and you can make it a positive experience, then this might be the right way to go.

If you have the choice as to what you want to do, you should take a day to decide and not rush it. Let it sit overnight then let your work know what you prefer to do the next day, however no later than this. Remember it has happened, the decision has been made, the sooner you start the ADAPT process, the sooner you can move on.

On a minor point, the date of your redundancy or lay off will be stated in your payout/package, so make sure that is accurate or aligned to any option you have been given to 'stay or go'.

So its happened, you have just been given the news that your job no longer exists and you will need to look elsewhere. It's a tough time. It's a confusing time.

<u>Send out your SOS (Significant Other Support)</u>

One of the key power moves is to as soon as it happens, send out an SOS.

SOS stands for 'significant other support'. Who is your SOS? Who are your 'first responders?'

Who is your support crew, your Go to people to be there for you? Whether it be family and friends, your work colleagues, a coach, a professional human resources or career counsellor, a psychologist, we all need our SOS.

I'm not a psychologist or a professional HR/careers specialist, but I am a coach with experience in what you are going through. I know that I leaned on a number of people to get me through my own experiences, not just the 'first responders' who I called as soon as it happened and were there with unconditional love and support but the people who were still there for me 3, 6 and 12 months later. And they know who they are.

There's definitely no shame in reaching out for professional help in these circumstances and remember to be discerning who you choose, who can serve you best in this moment.

Whether it be outplacement support, career planners, job seeking support or the practical counsel from mentors, coaches and people who know you and respect you. So gather the troops, you are going to need them and they will help to fast track you – but choose wisely.

A short phone call or email to them to let them know what's happened giving them the facts and asking for a time to catch up or see them. Depending who you are talking to and how well they know you, it's better initially to keep to the facts and try and contain your emotions as it is usually easier for someone to help you at that point.

Find one person who you can vent to who will hear you out, no judgement and go for it emotionally and express what you want to say, how you feel, whatever you need to.

In the makeup of your SOS team it is important to have diversity. Include a person who you can vent to without judgement, some professional 'helpful' people who know you and respect you and ideally a complete stranger (i.e. a coach, career strategist, out placement support) who can focus you on the practical steps to get you through.

When stuff happens in our life, it is sometimes hard to find the right people to talk about it to.

But talking things out, makes a difference. A big difference.

I'm a natural introvert, so I don't naturally feel the need to talk out aloud so much as I do to reflect inwards on things as they happen to me or around me. Alone time works well for me. But my SOS team helped me greatly by being there as a sounding board as and when I needed them. As a coach, I am now doing this for other people as well and it is rewarding to be part of someone's journey through this significant change and seeing them grow and flourish.

You might feel the same or on the other hand, get energised in sharing what's going on for you with others and it helps to talk things through.

Both ways are right, I honestly think we need a bit of both when we are confronted with challenges in our lives.

As a sidenote, my boss who delivered the message to me, remains a friend and a key contact for me and continues to be part of my network because of the way we both handled the situation.

<u>The emotional rollercoaster</u>

How did it happen for you?

How do you feel about what just happened? Whatever you feel is real. There will be an emotional response to the event that you need to acknowledge and be aware of.

But its helpful to be aware of your emotions as they will be responsible for your approach and your response if you are not careful.

So what do you feel?

Most common reactions are, but not limited to;

You may feel disrupted

It can be disruptive;

- To our ability to provide for our family and pay the bills
- To our wealth building or financial security
- To our dreams and our plans
- To our self worth and identity
- To our desire for a career path and promotion
- To our community connections, friends and co-workers
- To our psyche and what we believe about ourselves
- To our lives and those around us
- To any sense of certainty that has now disappeared.

You may feel derailed

It can feel like your plans have been derailed, you know that career that you had all mapped out and someone just sent it off its tracks in a 5-minute conversation.

You may feel disappointed

It can disappoint you that something you really liked has been taken away from you.

You may feel dismayed or confused

It may make you want to question that integrity and personal intentions and responsibilities of the people and the business you worked for. Its hard not to, because it might be completely out of the blue for you. It makes you ask 'why me' and 'its not fair'.

You may feel terrified

Not knowing what you are going to do.

You may feel humiliated

You worry about what people are going to say about you.

You may feel guilty

Like its all your fault and there was stuff you could have done to avoid it, but you didn't.

You may feel like you have let yourself and others down

You just weren't good enough.

And on the reverse side:

You may feel relief

It's a job you don't like or has hit a dead end for you, then this life event can be a huge relief and a welcome relief.

You may feel released

There something about a decision being made for you that can be quite liberating and be like lifting a major weight off your shoulders.

Everyone is different and it will affect us all differently. That's Ok whatever it is.

PART

We must say goodbye to the old and unplug from the current workplace.

PART stands for:

Pause and get some perspective

Approach

Reaction (yours and others)

Take care of your needs

This next step usually starts anywhere from straight after you heard the news to the following few weeks.

It is a critical stage and is where the realisation of what just happened, starts to sink in.

It is not just about now handling some of the logistics i.e. the paperwork etc., but also needing to deal with the mental and emotional detachment from your job, workplace, colleagues and a community that you spent a lot of time with.

This can be hard to do, so care is required at this stage.

Your job at this stage is to unplug from your old job, in readiness for the new.

- Unplug from the people
- Unplug from the work itself
- Unplug from the routine i.e. the daily commute
- Unplug from the financial security of that job
- Unplug from your identity linked to that job

It can be particularly hard if your job was with people who are your friends and the people that you hang out with – your social network.

What is important now, is to redefine how you will stay in touch with them. This will take some effort on both side to stay in touch and its natural that when the nature of relationships change, some will drop off and others will remain. This can be really hard and confusing at the time, but be prepared for it and let things taking their natural course. You can always go back and reconnect with work colleagues in the future, but let the relationships just simmer for a bit, whilst you get back on your feet.

Pause and get some perspective

Take a moment and develop an empowering perspective on what's just happened.

<u>Pause</u>

It's a time for some self reflection. This is a mental and emotional challenge and the bit that most of us feel is hard to do when faced with this event.

It may have been several hours or few days since you got the news that your job no longer exists.

You may be feeling a myriad of emotions from confusion to anger, from devastation to liberation.

It's important that you pause and take a breath. Take a moment. Take a day or two or several days even, just to pause and be OK with not taking any action. It's a big change, but its not insurmountable.

When we pause, we give our unconscious mind a chance to be heard. We turn off the noise around us, the overload of information and the reactions and we give ourselves a chance to centre ourselves and just stand in the truth of what just happened.

This is where mindfulness and meditation are very powerful and helpful in this moment.

The myth of being able to still your mind to listen to your thoughts is just that – a myth. Its not possible to still your mind, but it is possible to quieten it – to turn down the volume a bit.

Finding a place of contemplation whether it be meditation or walking or exercise – anything that allows you to be gentle to yourself can have enormous benefit to your reducing stress levels and any feelings of anxiety or overwhelm. If going to the gym and doing a tough workout helps, then do that! If taking a walk works, do that. If heading off on a long weekend away works for you, then do that.

This your time. This is all about you. But you need to create a good environment for yourself. A place to pause for as long as you need.

During this time, here's some reflection questions to ask yourself.

- Am I OK?
- What's the truth about this situation I'm in?
- What's in my control right now? What can I let go for now?
- What am I grateful for right now in my life?
- What do I truly value in my life and for my future?

Writing down what you feel and discover during the time of Pause, will be helpful and give you the ability to move past some of the fear you may be facing about your future. It's not necessarily thoughts you need to share with others. In the Pause, we just turn inwards and try to listen to what our inner voice or our intuition is telling us.

Perspective

As the coin toss analogy earlier infers, you are in charge of the perspective you give to this event. What you call it, will make a difference. Be mindful of the meaning you place on this event in your life. We need to assign a constructive meaning to it and your choice of language is very powerful.

- As an example, are you telling people that your career will take a 'dive' or just a slight 'dip' at the moment. See the difference?
- Are you telling people that you feel violated and used or are you telling yourself and others, that its was time to move on and now you can.
- Are you telling people that it was all your fault or are you telling yourself and others that it is was the company's decision and nothing you could do about it, so you are focussing on the future.

It's time to catch your thinking and what you are actually saying about the event and if needed reframe it in a way that is an empowering statement. One that supports you, not one that keeps you locked away in fear, desperation and despondency.

Know that whatever the 'story' you are telling **yourself** about what happened is what you are telling **others**.

Over the next few days, weeks and months, you will be asked about it a lot and if the perspective or story you have on the event is disempowering, every time you are asked about it, you will be dragged back into the negativity of the event, rather than being able to keep your feet grounded in the progress you have made, where they are and focused on your future.

There is no doubt that losing your job can be a **disruptive** moment. Having something that you were familiar with taken away from you (frankly whether you liked it or not), creates disruption. That's natural.

But the flip side, is that it can also be a **defining** moment. A moment that shines a light on your life and shows up something new. Something new about you, some new insight, sets the tone for new decisions, new behaviours and new ways of doing things.

- For some people it will mean very little – it will just be a little inconvenient and they can move on easily.
- For some people, it will be devastating and stop them in the tracks (at least for a moment).
- And for others, it will be an incredibly liberating moment and a very positive step into their new future

Becoming self aware of what meaning you are placing on this event and getting an empowering perspective is important. I found it really helpful to use what I call my 'Perspective Line'.

On this line there is a continuum of emotional meanings and being able to honestly admit what you and how you are thinking is a powerful starting point.

Try this exercise: Where are you on the 'perspective line' in regard to your recent job loss?

The Perspective Line

| Incredibly devastating | A little inconvenient | Awesomely liberating |

It doesn't matter where you place yourself on this line. The important point is that you become aware and honest about where you are starting from. This is your perspective after all.

And here's the good news – where you may start on this continuum, may not necessarily be where you end up. This means your perspective may change, evolve as you get stronger and clearer in yourself and perhaps regain some of your footing back to solid ground.

Over the course of my interviews with people who have been through this and my own personal experience, it has proven the case, that we tend to move left and right on The Perspective Line at times all the way through this situation. That's expected.

Whilst you may not find yourself at the extreme ends, you may well fluctuate from feeling devastated and demoralised about the situation, to some feelings of liberating and genuine excitements.

And you get to decide what the meaning or the perspective is. It doesn't matter what others think it might mean. This is your call. You make it.

A job loss is a temporary setback – it is not a sign that your dreams are on the ropes.

They are still intact and in play – the pathway to your success has just taken a curve.

John Lees, UK-based career strategies and author of How to Get a Job You Love" says "getting laid off is a manageable setback on the scale of human experience".

It's not game over. It might just be that all you have to do is restart the game.

<u>There's no shame and no room for blame</u>

There is never ever a need or a reason to feel ashamed or let anyone else shame us, anytime but specifically in this circumstance when we are told that our job no longer exists.

Brene Brown, #1 New York Times Best Seller and self proclaimed 'shame researcher' defines shame as follows;

"Shame is basically the fear of being unlovable – it's the total opposite of owning our story and feeling worthy… Shame is the intensely painful feeling or experience of believing that we are flawed and therefore unworthy of love and belonging".

You may have heard or read about the key premise that we are all enough… just the way we are.

Just because your job no longer exists, doesn't mean you don't belong and are not worthy just as you are.

By having something not work out just the way you intended or even after you have worked really hard for it, there is never any shame.

This is not a time to be ashamed of your 'under employment' right now. As far as we know, this could be the best thing to ever happen to you and this is the start of something completely new for you.

The problem comes from when our ego shows up and tells us our identity is all about what we have achieved, our status, our accomplishments. When you lose your job, you do lose the identity of you with that job, but you don't lose you.

Hanging onto your old identity will not serve you.

But there is no need to completely start again. If you were a middle manager leading teams, you are still a middle manager leading teams. If you are a product marketing expert, you are still a product marketing expert. If you are a designer, then you are still a designer.

Resist the urge to throw 'the baby out with the bathwater' just because one job has ended, doesn't mean your career in that field is over. Keep what is good about your credentials and experience and apply it to the new role.

For some people, they will want to now try something completely new – maybe go into business for themselves, but all those skills and experience are transferable, so take them with you. Be proud of them and you will bring more value to your next venture.

Don't leave it all behind.

<u>Ditch the ego – they CAN do it without you.</u>

Here's a perspective for you. No one is indispensable.

Sure it's inconvenient when the person who knows the most about something leaves the company or organisation, under any circumstances but it is temporary. Someone will fill that knowledge or skill gap.

The business will go on without you. You are replaceable.

Rest assured, someone else will be able to pick up whatever it is you left half done, your tasks, those unwritten meeting minutes you may not have done yet, the project meetings scheduled for next week that you will no longer be there for.

Life will go on in the company without you. It will not stop, it might slow down for a bit, as the organisation makes the necessary internal changes on what happens to your role, but it will go on.

So don't make the mistake of worrying about that. You are not going to be there. The decision has been made.

It's natural for our ego to take a bit of a hit when you are told you are no longer required. Our egos thrive on relevance and importance and right now in this moment, you are not as relevant nor as important to the company's success as you used to be.

That can hurt. But it is our ego talking and it is not helpful to dwell on this.

Ditch your ego – of course someone else could do what you were doing, but they definitely won't do it the way you did it. ☺

It's no longer your job to manage and run all the tasks you were looking after.

Just leave professionally and let your 'ex' worry about all of that.

Approach

Be professional, pragmatic, positive, pro-active and practical.

Your approach is everything, because this is about ensuring you set yourself up in the best light.

Who have you become in this situation? Are you at your best or worse in these situations? This is an interesting time for you to see how you do handle crises and can be one of the most liberating outcomes from the situation. At this time, you can find out a lot about who you are as a person and a leader.

Remember your job is to deal with what's happening right now, you don't have to like it!

If you can establish a calm and collected approach at this point, it will help when you choose to start searching for another job. It is unadvisable to get in front of a recruiter until your emotions are somewhat under control, so finding a sense of calm will help.

If you remain overcome with emotion, it is probably an indication that means you need to take some more time and work through things before you jump in and start the job seeking. This is OK if that happens, just give yourself a bit more time.

<u>Be professional – don't bad mouth your 'ex'</u>

Be professional. It will stand you in good stead. It might feel pretty hard to do so, particularly if you are feeling hurt and betrayed by the situation. However, this one strategy will pay off in the long term.

Leave the door open at your organization by acting professionally and refraining from openly commenting on any specific person or their involvement in the situation or their behavior.

There is zero to gain in speaking badly of your ex employer or organization in the after math of being told your job no longer exists.

Refrain from being part of rumors and gossip or derogatory comments. Again you may not be feeling all that happy about the situation and still be struggling with why it happened to you, but it will not help you to engage in negativity with others, particularly anyone in your current workplace.

Refrain from commenting on social media at this time about your job loss. Full stop. End of sentence.

You are in the midst of a relationship break up and the healing will begin when you can see your 'ex' without a charge and you can put your energy into focusing forward. For some people, it helps to 'forgive' the other party, but to do this you need to do so not expecting any response from them. It is unlikely you will be satisfied if you do.

Finally, this is not a point scoring or time for defamation. Be focused on the path forward, not looking backwards.

<u>Be pragmatic - accept that it is personal</u>

Know this. When you are told your job no longer exists, of course it's personal. It's personal to you and personal to your position or the work that you did at least. It can happen to anyone but it happened to you.

As John Lees from 'How to Get a Job You Love' says "it's a rejection – the company is saying,' We don't need you. We can manage without you. It feels personal".

It's incredibly personal to you, it may not be so to your company. To them, it may be a clinical decision i.e. the need to cut heads and lower wage costs or perhaps a strategic shift to move in another direction and seek to find other skill sets.

It's just another form of a relationship break up. You are no longer going to see each other every work day. You are going to go your separate ways. It's going to be hard and there may well be tears, but the fact is the relationship as you knew it is over.

Of course it's personal – it is about you, it happened to you.

<u>Be positive - remind yourself what you are good at.</u>

Losing your job or having it taken away from you will likely create a 'self esteem' hit.

Why? Because we think that our self esteem is linked to what we have achieved and naturally then, the identity we have created from the job we have, the job title we have worked hard to get, the status and salary our position holds within a company.

It's hard not to think this way, but the truth is that we need to understand, particularly at times exactly such as these, that our identity or self esteem has NOTHING to do with what we have achieved. It has EVERYTHING to do with who we are as a person.

Right now, you may have been on a specific career trajectory and had plans for moving up in an organisation and perhaps even reaching the top job. To do this, you must be achieving and delivering results and demonstrating your effective leadership and communication skills.

Or at this time, you may have been working in a role that really suited you and your lifestyle, afforded you some flexibility and freedom that worked for you and your personal life and family and it was good and comfortable.

Or it could be that you were in a role, that you no longer enjoyed and hoping that the next step would become obvious and available to you so you could move on in the near future to something you felt was more aligned to what you wanted and who you are.

In all the above cases, there must be some things that you do (or did) that you were uniquely good at and it is really important that at this time, you remind yourself of exactly what they are.

Why? Because it will be easy for you to focus on what may seem to be your 'lack' or the 'things you got wrong' as an explanation as to why you were the one who was told that your job no longer exists. Because what just happened to you may not make much sense to you right now, your brain will go and try and scramble some sense and come up with an explanation, which may have nothing to do with the truth.

Let me share with you how this played out for me. When I was told my job no longer existed, and after some initial reactions, negative and positive, the best and most empowering action I took, was to ask my SOS team, which included in my case people I reported to and people who reported to me, this question:

"What am I good at again? I've forgotten!"

It might sound like one of those dumb questions, but it was easily the most charged (powerful) questions I could ask at that time, because of what happened next.

I had people shower me with recognition and gratitude for my skills and talents and the impact I have had. I was so blown away by the kind and generous comments that I wrote them all down and titled it 'The Things I Am Good At' list and stuck them up on my desk (at home now ☺) and I still look at them from time to time as an encouraging reminder.

It said things like writing, leading teams, creativity, projects, giving, sharing what I learn with others, resilience, visionary and being the world's fastest report writer. These are the things that my teams and my colleagues and bosses all valued in me. This list was a life saver and I still have it on my desk today.

It is hard to write this list for yourself, but great if you can. So ask others and it will help you keep your mind on the truth of what's great about you and help you not to get side-tracked down a path of feeling you 'were not enough' for the job or the company.

It's a simple action to take, but very powerful.

<u>Be pro-active – craft your own story and tell it in less than 30 seconds</u>

One of the most important and helpful things you can do is to craft your response or your story as to what has just happened for you and what it means.

Do you know how many times you get asked in a social situation or meeting new people, is 'what do you do?'

Well one of your power moves is to get a great powerful response to that one question "so (insert name) What do you do?"

And its great to keep it short and sweet, because nobody wants to hear your long and winding story, they are more interested in where you are right now and where you are heading.

I want you to be truthful and open, but to speak an empowering story, not one that keeps you locked into being a victim of circumstance.

I like the goal of being able to say your story in under 30 seconds. Here's some examples:

"Recently I was told my job no longer existed and whilst it was a shock because I loved what I was doing, it has given me a chance to refocus on finding a role now that pursues my leadership skills and managing small teams."

"I was just told recently that my job is finishing up in 4 weeks because the company is restructuring, so I am looking at my options and working out which is the right move for me".

"I'm taking a career break at the moment, after being told my job no longer existed and looking after my health and recharging the batteries. Then I am going to investigate an option to work for myself doing what I really love …"

"Well, I got some tough news recently that my job no longer exists and I just need to find another role asap, so I can keep the income coming in. I am looking for roles in …… So you have any suggestions or people I should be talking to please?"

So we don't have to articulate over and over again how hurt we may feel or confused or even stuck. By having a short statement about where we are and what we are looking for, it will help us feel more positive and to be honest, make 'answering' that dreaded question of 'What do you do' a whole lot less stressful. Rehearsing this answer over and over again, it will become automatic and will help keep you in a positive state of mind.

To help you become aware of what you really feel this is meaning for you, take the following exercise to 'craft own story'.

<u>Exercise: Craft Your Own Story</u>

Step 1 - Write down your answers to the question in each of the columns

Step 2 – Notice which column resonates with you more

Step 3 – Take the statements from each column and weave a 30 second story that you feel accurately and honestly represents where you are at the moment and that feels empowering to say.

	It feels devastating because…	It feels a little inconvenient because…	It feels liberating because…
Example	The work hours I had on my job really worked for my family situation	I might have to do some more training	On the next job, I'll look for somewhere that has more opportunities for promotion
Your answer…			

Repeat the exercise as you wish. The end goal here is having more responses in the 'it feels liberating' column as you move your way through handling this event.

Keep your 30 second story handy and memorise it, so you feel confident and at ease responding in the moment to people who will ask you what do you do, when you are out of work. It will be a whole lot easier to answer with your pre-prepared 30 second authentic answer.

<u>Be practical – cease outsourcing your career to someone else</u>

This power move is confronting.

If you are feeling like you have been let down by your boss or your company/organisation, you thought that you were on a track for a promotion, not being told you are no longer required, then here's the question to ask yourself

At what point, did you decide to outsource your career development to the company you work for? Have you been the one driving your career decisions or did you just assume it would happen.

This is a tough lesson to learn, but the fact is you are responsible for your career and it is up to you to stay on top of what you need to do to get that promotion you no doubt deserve.

As Steve Jobs says, "the world is made up of decisions that are made by people who don't know any more than you" If that's true, then its possible that the people you worked for, may not have been the best people to represent your career interests or perhaps you were not realistic about them or did not make your intentions clear to them, so they could not support your goals as you wanted them to.

From here, be your own career manager. That's your job – it always will be.

Reaction (yours and others)

Prepare yourself.

Your reaction is your reality and its important as we have just discussed to react in a way that is aligned with you in a way that is effective for you.

You would not be mistaken to think that losing your job is all about you! But in fact, you may find that one of your biggest challenges is to handle the reaction of others to your news.

This is something that took me by surprise I must admit.

This change can make others feel uncomfortable and unsure to know what to say to you, so be prepared for this and know it is not your job to make them feel comfortable, although that is what tends to happen.

Some people will avoid you altogether – not because they don' t care about you and your future, but they really don't know what to say to you.

However, some people will simply avoid you – for whatever their reason – it could be anything. Don't worry about these people – move on.

Some people will surprisingly make it all about them and how it affects them ☺. This is interesting, as often it is a coping mechanism on their part and you need to be very aware not to take offence at their lack of sensitivity.

Some people will offer their support and reach out to you.

Some people will immediately want to know what your plans are and what you are going to do next. This can be from an interest and care point of view but also again, it can be a comfort seeking thought on their part. These people will feel better if they know you have it all together.

Some people will be want to dive into the negatives with you and are the ones who jump on the 'injustice' of it all and want to bad mouth all the people involved. This is neither helpful to you or the situation and its going to be really important that you excuse yourself from these conversations as soon as they start.

Be honest in talking with others but be aware, who you are talking to and their motivation.

You will need to provide re-assurance to others, just be ready for it.

My suggestion is to have a short and to the point response such as:

"Yes it was a shock, but I'm focusing now on the options in front of me…"

This is where crafting your own story and having an empowering perspective will work for you and for those around you.

Take care of you

Your wellbeing is well 'everything'.

This is your time to take care of yourself. Make it about you, because it is about you.

If we are in good health, we will be better able to cope with the stress of losing and 'finding' a new job.

This is a great time to reconnect with your health goals and take up some extra effort to get into shape or have more rest. Whatever you need.

Mindful and meditation practices are a great way to stay centred and aware of yourself and are a great stress reduction tactic.

There's plenty of information on the internet and free apps on meditations and mindfulness that you can access.

For some people they will have an immediate priority such as to get another job because there are bills to pay and a family to support or financial commitments to keep. That is expected and should be honoured and appropriate action taken.

For others, who can create some breathing space, the best thing they can do is to take some time out and look after their health and wellbeing. This may mean taking a few days, few weeks off and rest and recuperate – physically, emotionally and mentally. This is very powerful and will give you an opportunity to pause and get a perspective on what just happened and recharge ready for the next steps.

For myself, I gave permission to take 12 months to work it out and decided not to jump into the first thing I thought of. I called this my 'gap year'.

I travelled, started writing as a creative outlet and focused on getting my health in order. Within this time, I realised that I wanted to take all my experience and expertise and help others through the same situation and also that I was going to establish a coaching practice with the view of having a business that I could work from anywhere and anytime.

Here's what others said were the most important things for them to do at this time.

"My health is everything – I am going to focus on that"

"I am going to take a breather / a break and think about what I really want to do"

"I am going to take stock financially and work out what I really need"

"I am going to reach out to my mates and hang out with them for awhile"

RESTART

We must get ready and make room for the new.

RESTART stands for:

Renew your focus

Explore all options

Seek more information

Take stock financially

Access all available resources

Resume and social profiles

Treat it like a project

Renew your focus

Be intentional.

The most important thing you can do at this point is be focused and intentional about what you want.

If you don't know what you want, then this is the time to seek some help. Whether it be a career counsellor, colleagues or a coach, just know that the clearer you are on what you want, the more likely you will know what action to take and more likely you will be able to create your new reality.

Setting a clear intention and backed by focus and commitment is now what is required.

To be focused, means;

1. Set your sights on what you do want to happen, not what you don't want to happen.
2. Be disciplined with your time.
3. Honor this moment – in this moment you have an issue you need to resolve, so put 100% of your attention and energy into it.

<u>Do a values check</u>

A value or values, according to The Oxford Dictionary, can be defined as:

"the regard that something is held to deserve, the importance, worth or usefulness of something" or "principles or standards of behavior: one's judgment of what is important in life".

At a catch up lunch, I asked a colleague of mine, Paul who had recently been told his job longer existed as to what he did that was the most important thing he did, he was quick to reply.

Paul said, "I make my decisions based on my values. So I used this opportunity to check in with what my values were and to ensure that I was making my next career move, in alignment with what my values were:

Do you know what your values are?

Have you ever taken the time to think about, even list them out?

If you are not sure of what values are important to you, then it's a good time to find that out. If you already do have an idea of what they are, it's a good opportunity to revisit them and update if necessary.

Our values can change over time. The core list may stay the same, but the priority order of our values can definitely change given a particular life event or life stage we are going through.

Values can be anything such as charity, accomplishment, achievement, decisiveness, clarity, joy, leadership, integrity, fun and so on.

Explore all options

Anything is possible, avoid the bounce - don't jump too early.

As I mentioned at the start of this book, the best piece of advice I received was from John Turner at Talent 2, was to go and research at least 3 options. He actually gave me this exercise to do.

On a piece of paper, make a list of 3 options as to what you might want to do and list them.

When I went to talk to people and they asked me what my plans were, I was able to reel off the list of these 3 and then something amazing happened. John told me this was going to happen and it did just as he described.

People would fill in more options for me. They would tell me what I was not seeing or couldn't see for myself and it was remarkable and very helpful. Soon I had my list of three, plus three – four more options that other people gave to me.

For me, my first three things were:

1. Get my same job but with another organization
2. Contract for awhile and not take on a full time role
3. Set up my own business and work for myself

When I talked with others and showed them my list, the things that were added were:

4. Become CEO of a small not for profit
5. Be a writer, because I love writing so much
6. Do more coaching
7. Become a personal project manager for individuals and entrepreneurs.

Helpful? Yes.

So its not always going to be the first thing you might think of that is the right one. Being able to just hold the space open for awhile and getting that invaluable input from others made all the difference.

For me, instead of jumping into the first thing I thought of i.e. find a similar job, but in a different organization, I ended up looking at a broader range of options and taking the best bits of the ones I liked the most and combining them into a compelling vision of what I really wanted to do.

I knew that part of the whisper I ignored was that I really wanted to establish my own business that serves others on a global scale by helping them with projects. This came from acknowledgment that 'projects are in my DNA' and I am passionate about projects that can make a real difference. So I knew this, but was terrified at the prospect and uncertainty that comes from leaving the workforce and a steady paycheck to being out on my own.

I had to weigh up what was most important to me (my values) and how passionate I was to put in to get the results I so wanted and deserved.

Don't ignore the whisper

Before you go and take the next job or make your next career move, take some time to consider whether there is a bigger meaning to this event in your life? Is it telling you something?

I was someone who ignored the whisper of my soul telling me its was time to go and do my thing.

As you are evaluating all your options, consider spending time finding or reconnecting with your purpose. What are you good at? What brings you joy? What can you do that brings value?

Don't make a career plan, make a plan about what experiences, growth or contribution you want to make. Vishen Lakhiani, CEO Mindvalley developed these 3 simple, but important questions to ask each and every person that works for him or is part of his business circle.

He calls it the '3 most important questions'. You can find Vishen and the 3 most important questions on YouTube (https://www.youtube.com/watch?v=f8eU5Pc-y0g).

Take the exercise from Vishen:

On a piece of paper, draw up three columns or use Vishen's template provided.

Ask yourself what experiences do I want to have?

What growth do I want to have?

What contribution do I want to make?

And the idea is to do this quickly, don't over think it. You can always come back to it and revise and update.

When I did this exercise and it is still up above my desk, it became obvious to me that I wanted a collection of experiences, a range of personal growth challenges and above all else, to make a clear and impactful contribution back to the planet doing what I love and serving others.

This exercise was a key power move for getting clear on what I wanted and my decision to build my own project coaching business to serve others. I highly recommend you do this exercise and do it with your family and friends as well.

EXPERIENCES	GROWTH	CONTRIBUTION

mindvalley

Seek more information

Get the information you need to make great decisions.

Once you have established your short list of options, it is now time to do some research into each option. The purpose here is get enough information for you to rule that option either in or out.

A great outcome at this stage, is that you rule out some options, but only after you have investigated them. A new option such as setting up a new business can be pretty radical and would be easy to dismiss early on, but resist this if you know it could be a great option for you.

Some ideas need more incubation than others. The timing might be off, but the idea still has some merit, so don't dismiss it.

Keep your options open, after all this is an amazing time for you. A time that has created space for you to look at what you really want.

Some options may start to look very appealing, but maybe the time is not right for you.

Some options may be more long term and will require a number of steps, but its possible you can start now and have a commitment to just start something new, even whilst you seek to get another job.

And sometimes we need to massage some of the options to make them more compelling.

Here's a useful exercise to compare the options available to you, once you have identified them.

Using the comparison grid on the next page, there are 4 squares.

Square # 1 – means the option has high appeal and low effort

Square # 2 – means the option has high appeal and high effort

Square # 3 – means the option has low appeal and high effort

Square # 4 – means the option has low appeal and low effort.

Which is the best square for you?

If we honestly evaluate each option available to us by placing it in the most relevant square, this grid can start to give us a clearer picture of how the options compare with each other.

Obviously we want to avoid, anything that fits into Square 3 and aim to find an option that is either in Square 1 or Square 2.

Exercise: Take the short list of options available to you and plot them onto the grid. I have shown you what my grid looked like for all the options I had at the time as an example.

After completing the grid, does it give you a clearer picture of all your options and how they compare? If there is something in a square others than #1 or #2, how can you adjust it to make it have more appeal or take less effort, so it will become a more compelling option?

What are all my options?

Set up my own passion
based business and work
for myself

Do more
professional
coaching

Become a
professional writer

2   1

Become a CEO of a small
not for profit

Get my same job back but
with another organisation

Become a personal project
manager for individuals and
entrepreneurs

Appeal

Contract for awhile and
not take on a full time role

4   3

Switch to a completely
new career

Take an alternative role in
the same company at a
lower salary

High   Low

Effort

"If the ladder is not leaning against the right wall, every step

we take just gets us to the wrong place faster"

Stephen Covey

Take stock financially

Get clear on what you have and what you need.

Everyone's situation is different, but to get clear on your financial situation and your goals is imperative at this point.

This book is not about giving you financial advice, but what I will say, that using this time to regroup around your financial goals and your intentions for the future is one of the most important actions you can take.

So seek out advice from your financial advisor and be clear about where you stand financially and what you need to put into place in the short and long term.

Access all available resources

You are not alone #Yana. Remember that.

There is a lot of support and resources available to you.

From your organisation:

- Outplacement support – your organisation may have provided this to you. If so, utilise all the available services.

From colleagues:

- Ask your colleagues for introductions to key people in other organisations or recruiters that may be able to assist. Every effort should be put into maintaining your existing network as well as growing it by meeting new people and there is nothing more powerful that getting recommended or introduced to someone, by someone who knows you very well.

From independent advice:

- Seek out career counsellors, business advisors and mentors or a coach to get some independent perspective. The independent nature of advice at this point is really important to balance out the well wishes of people who are closest to you. Again we are looking to get a balanced view of all our options, so finding someone to talk to you outside of your immediate family and friends is critical.

Use your networks wisely. Most people will be more than happy to provide you with the support you need and to make referrals to other people as needed if you make it easy for them to help you.

The clearer you are on what you want or need, the easier it is for people to provide you with that assistance.

Resume and social profiles

Look up and see that the job seeking world is constantly changing.

Updating your resume or CV is a practical action to take. Get some advice if you are not sure what to include or exclude. There is plenty of online advice available to you for free and once its updated, you can send it off to some very cost effective platforms such as Fiverr for formatting for around $5 - $10 USD. No need to spend big dollars on the physical formatting of your resume, but it should look as professional as you can make it.

Your social profiles are critical now. Whether you are a social media expert or a complete newbie, having online profiles is critical. That is how people will find your and know that your new status regarding your employment.

Other than the main socials such as Facebook and Linked in for example, it will be important to have an online presence on the major job seeking sites as well. Set up accounts and upload your resume and create a profile. These do change over time, so a simple google search or recommendations from a professional in this field will help you know which ones are best for you.

The realities are that the job seeking world has changed significantly and you need to get up to speed quickly.

<u>Make age your advantage</u>

This is for the over 50's. Buying into ageism, will not help you – we have been around the grounds long enough to know better

If mindset is everything, then do not buy into the myth that age does matter.

If you think you are too young or too old, then you may well be.

Instead focus on bringing out all the experience and impact you have had in your roles and how you can help the companies or organisations you want to work for

Treat it like a project

Start with the end in mind.

I might be a bit biased here, but I think pulling together a strategy, knowing what actions to take, putting in place some deadlines and a way of tracking your progress is a very effective way to navigate your way through where you are now to where you want to get to.

So I suggest you create a project called 'My next job role or career move'.

Some of you will already know how a project works and is put together, and the key is to keep it as simple as possible.

It's a good idea to start with the end in mind or other words, know what your end point or target is and work backwards to where you are today and that will give you good visibility of some key steps you need to take now to propel you forward.

Conclusion

Finding out that your job no longer exists has the potential to not only disrupt us, but completely derail our plans…if we let it.

By following through the three stages – ADAPT. PART. RESTART. and being mindful of being positive and future focused, you too will get through this and be able to move onto your exciting new future.

Don't let one decision stop you from living the life you deserve and desire.

May your ideal job or next step, find you and exceed your expectations.